VIOLINJUDY'S
BACK TO SCHOOL
PIANO PRE-READING

SUPPLEMENTARY SONGS
FOR BEGINNING PIANO LEARNERS

VERY FUN PIANO COLLECTION

Back To School by Judy Naillon
Copyright © 2023 ViolinJudy
www.violinjudy.com
ISBN: 978-1-960674-13-5

All Rights Reserved. This book or parts thereof may not be reproduced in any form, stored in any retrieval system, or transmitted in any form by any means-eletronic, mechanical, photocopy, recording, or otherwise – without prior written permission or the publisher, except as provided by copyright law.

VERY FUN PIANO LIBRARY

A Pre-Reading Piano Back To School is composed for beginning piano learners. Students using this book should be able to sit at the piano as many minutes as years of their age and recognize letters A-G and Numbers 1-5.

HOW TO USE QR CODES IN THIS BOOK:

HOW TO SCAN A QR CODE WITH AN IPHONE OR IPAD:

BOTH IPHONES AND IPADS HAVE A QR SCANNER BUILT INTO THE CAMERA.

1. WITH A QR CODE NEARBY, OPEN THE CAMERA ON YOUR IPHONE OR IPAD.

2. POSITION THE CAMERA SO THE QR CODE IS IN FRAME. YOUR IPHONE OR IPAD SHOULD SCAN IT AUTOMATICALLY, WITHOUT ANY INPUT NEEDED FROM YOU. ONCE IT SCANS THE CODE, A NOTIFICATION WILL APPEAR AT THE TOP OF YOUR SCREEN WITH THE LINK TO THE QR CODE'S CONTENT. TAP THIS AND YOU'LL BE BROUGHT TO IT.

HOW TO SCAN A QR CODE WITH AN ANDROID PHONE OR TABLET:

ANDROID DEVICES HAVE THE QR CODE SCANNER BUILT INTO THE CAMERA. HOWEVER, YOU MIGHT NEED TO OPEN A SPECIAL APP TO USE IT.

1. WITH A QR CODE NEARBY, OPEN THE CAMERA ON YOUR ANDROID DEVICE.

2. POSITION THE CAMERA SO THE QR CODE IS IN FRAME. YOUR ANDROID SHOULD SCAN IT AUTOMATICALLY, BUT IF IT DOESN'T, PRESS AND HOLD YOUR FINGER ON IT YOU'LL BE GIVEN THE LINK THAT THE QR CODE LEADS TO AND A CHOICE TO OPEN IT, COPY THE URL, OR SHARE IT.

TABLE OF CONTENTS

P.8 BACK TO SCHOOL

P.9 BACKPACK

P.10. RECESS

P.11 D, F & C WORKSHEET

P.12 SCHOOL DAYS

P.14 E, B, & C WORKSHEET

P.16 MARY`S MOUSE

P.17 D, G, & A WORKSHEET

P.18 TWINKLE TWINKLE LITTLE STAR

P.19 THE ITSY BITSY SPIDER

P. 20 ODE TO JOY

MUSIC RHYTHM FLASHCARDS

NOTE TO TEACHERS/PRACTICE PARENT:

Any beginning piano student can start in this book on any keyboard or real piano. The pacing of this series is slower than any other method book you will find. This allows younger beginners time to really learn to read music as well as play a wide variety of songs. When you establish a firm foundation of technic, listening skills and songs students know and like to play, you'll have a pianist who learns to love music! Playing pieces that are traditional and familiar, yet presented in a fun, fresh way engages the learner.

We start with floating off-the-staff notes in this book. The pacing is graded in a manner that the note reading will not be overwhelming. Finger numbers are placed above or below the noteheads as an aide and phase out in higher level books as we focus on note reading building one note at a time with exercises and pieces using only the notes we have learned. The advantage of having a printed book to send home with learners helps everyone remember what and how to practice. Even young children are often able to practice these without help after the first few lessons or by watching the included instructional videos. You may use this book as a pre-cursor or in conjunction with common method books for young beginners.

In this book you will find many
tools to help learn piano including
FUN songs and worksheets!

Pieces in this book are fun to play in group lessons as well!
Students who have successfully completed this book can look forward to more skills to learn and fun pieces to master in *A Very Fun Piano Collection*
available on Amazon!

DO'S AND DON'TS FOR PIANO:

WASH YOUR HANDS BEFORE YOU PLAY OR PRACTICE PIANO.

SIT TALL WITH YOUR FEET ON THE GROUND. IF THEY DON'T REACH, FIND SOME EMPTY BOXES TO REST YOUR FEET ON.

HOLD YOUR ARMS OUT SO THEY TOUCH THE FALLBOARD OF THE PIANO. IF YOUR ARMS ARE NOT PARALLEL WITH THE GROUND, FIND SOMETHING TO SIT ON TO MAKE YOURSELF TALLER LIKE A BOOSTER SEAT, CUSHION OR PILLOW.

LOOK AT WHERE YOUR FINGERS GO BEFORE YOU START THE PIECE

COUNT YOURSELF OFF BEFORE YOU START:
"1-2-READY-PLAY" OR "1-2-READY-GO"

KEEP YOUR FINGERS GLUED TO THE KEYS UNTIL YOU'RE DONE PLAYING

PLAYING ON A KEYBOARD IS FINE, HOWEVER STARTING ON A KEYBOARD THAT MAKES LOUD AND SOFT SOUNDS (HAS TOUCH RESPONSE) WILL HELP YOU MAKE MORE BEAUTIFUL MUSIC

IF YOU'RE FEELING WIGGLY SEE IF YOU CAN BALANCE A STUFFED ANIMAL ON YOUR HEAD FOR 10 SECONDS!

CURVE YOUR FINGERS WHEN YOU PLAY PIANO LIKE YOU'RE CATCHING A BUBBLE!

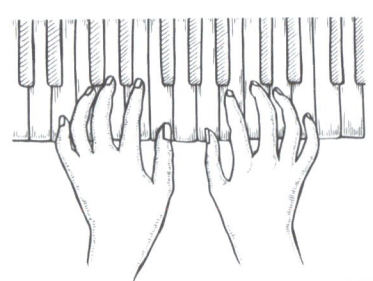

C. JUDY NAILLON 2021 WWW.VIOLINJUDY.COM

WHOLE NOTE	HALF NOTE	QUARTER NOTE	BASS CLEF
 "WHOLE NOTE HOLD IT" 4 BEATS	 "HOLD ME" 2 BEATS	 "QUARTER" 1 BEAT	 USE YOUR LEFT HAND TO PLAY THESE NOTES
THREE BLACK KEYS	**TWO BLACK KEYS**	**RIGHT HAND**	**TREBLE CLEF**
 USE YOUR "THREE YEARS OLD" FINGERS TO PLAY	 USE YOUR "TWO YEARS OLD" FINGERS TO PLAY	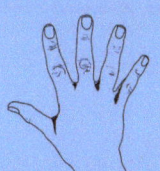 USE THIS HAND TO PLAY UP STEM NOTES	 USE YOUR RIGHT HAND TO PLAY THESE NOTES
LEFT HAND	**HALF REST**	**QUARTER REST**	**REPEAT SIGN**
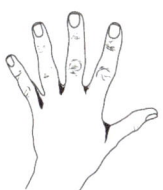 USE THIS HAND TO PLAY DOWN STEM NOTES	 HOLD 2 BEATS	 HOLD 1 BEAT	 PLAY AGAIN
DOUBLE BAR LINE	**EIGHTH NOTES**	**BAR LINE**	**DOTTED HALF NOTE**
 THE END OF THE PIECE	 RUNNING BUNNY = PLAY TWICE AS FAS AS QUARTER	CREATES MEASURES DON'T STOP!	 "HOLD ME PLEASE" THREE BEATS

C. JUDY NAILLON 2019 WWW.VIOLINJUDY.COM   PIANO BACK TO SCHOOL PREFACE

BACK TO SCHOOL!

Scan the QR code for a how-to video!

```
      3           4              
   2     2    3 3   3    2-  2-    3- - -
                  2                         
```
I CAN'T WAIT TO SEE MY FRIENDS,   BACK TO   SCHOOL!

```
      4              4
   3            3  3  3          3- 3-
   2     2               2                2- - -
                        2
```
FUN AND LEARNING NEVER END,   BACK TO   SCHOOL!

CAN YOU LABEL THESE RIGHT HAND FINGERS WITH NUMBERS 1,2,3,4,5?

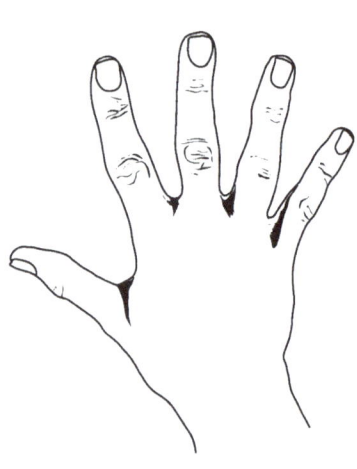

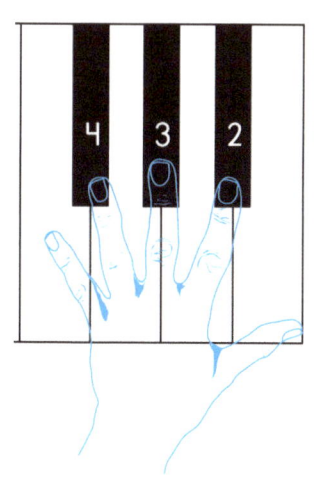

BACKPACK

Need help?

𝄢 | 2 2 | 2 2 | 3 - 3 - | 2 - 2 - |
           4 4 | 4 4 | | |

DO YOU HAVE YOUR   BACKPACK? DO YOU   HAVE YOUR   LUNCHBOX?

𝄢 | 2 2 | 2 2 | 3 - 3 - | 4 - - - ‖
           4 4 | 4 4 | |

YES I HAVE MY   BACKPACK AND A   HUG FOR   YOU!

CAN YOU LABEL THESE LEFT HAND FINGERS WITH NUMBERS 1,2,3,4,5 ?

RECESS

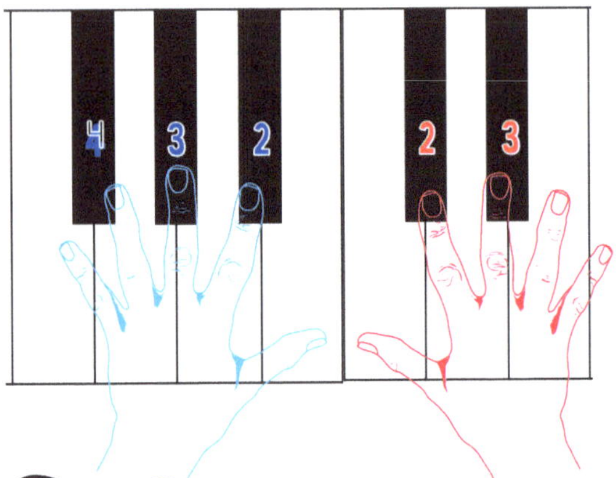

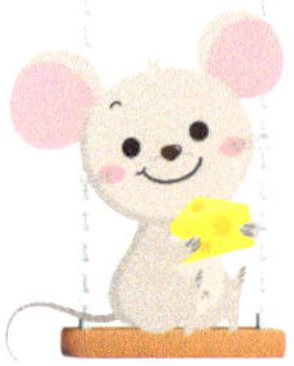

Watch a video here!

𝄢 2 | 2 | 𝄞 2 - 2 - | 3 - 3 - |
  3   3
  4 𝄽 4 𝄽

RECESS TIME!   RECESS TIME!   LET'S ALL   GO   PLAY!

𝄢   2 𝄽 | 2 𝄽 | 𝄞 3 - | 𝄢 4 𝄽 4 𝄽 ‖
  3   3   2 -
  4   4

JUMPING ROPE,   SWINGS & FRIENDS!   I   LOVE   RE -   CESS!

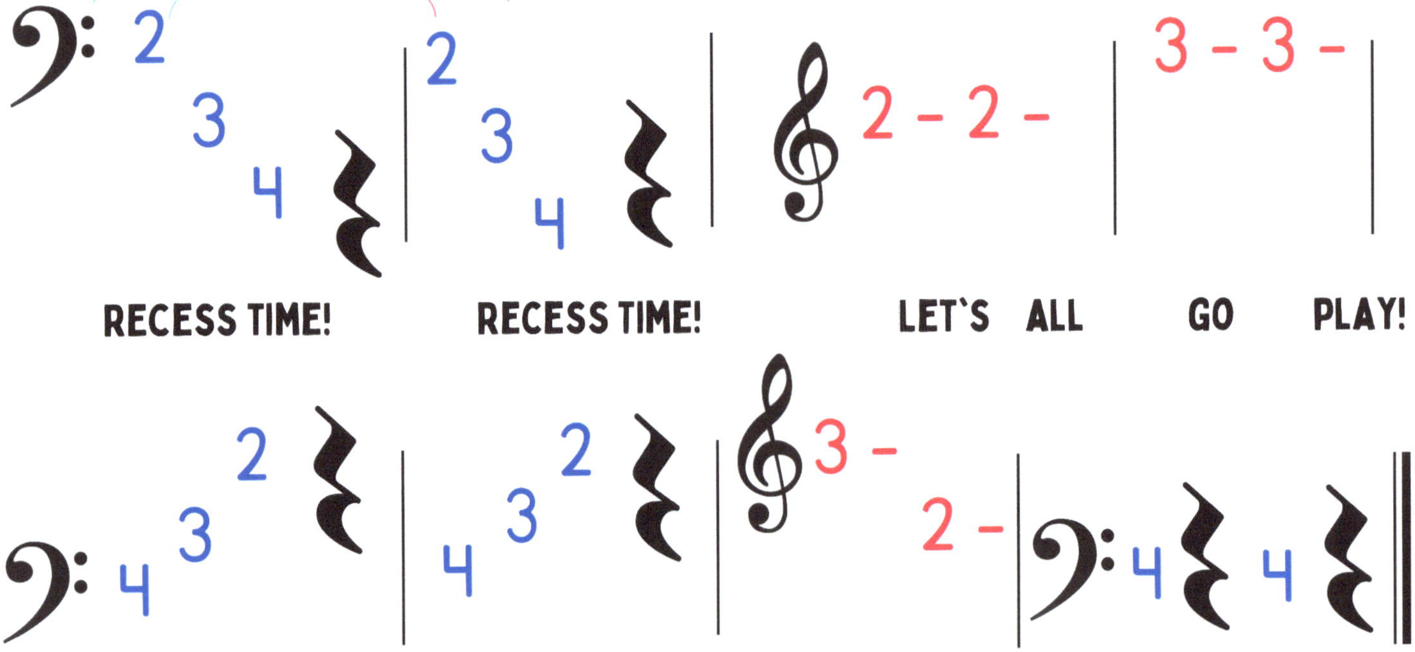

Can you label the missing fingers?

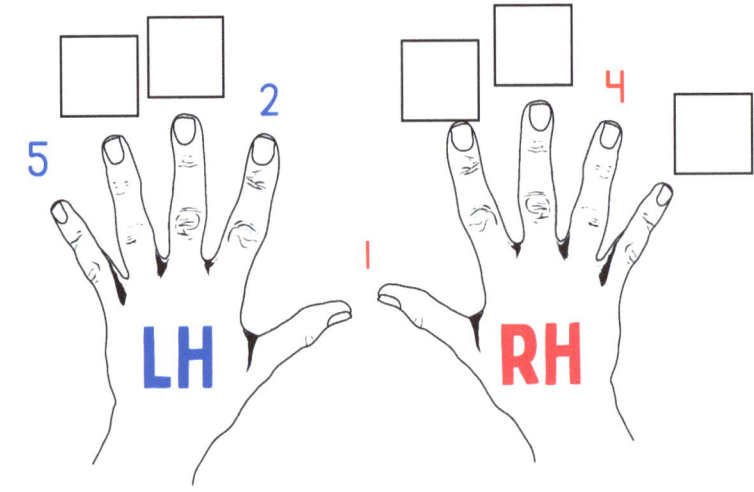

COLOR ALL THE D`S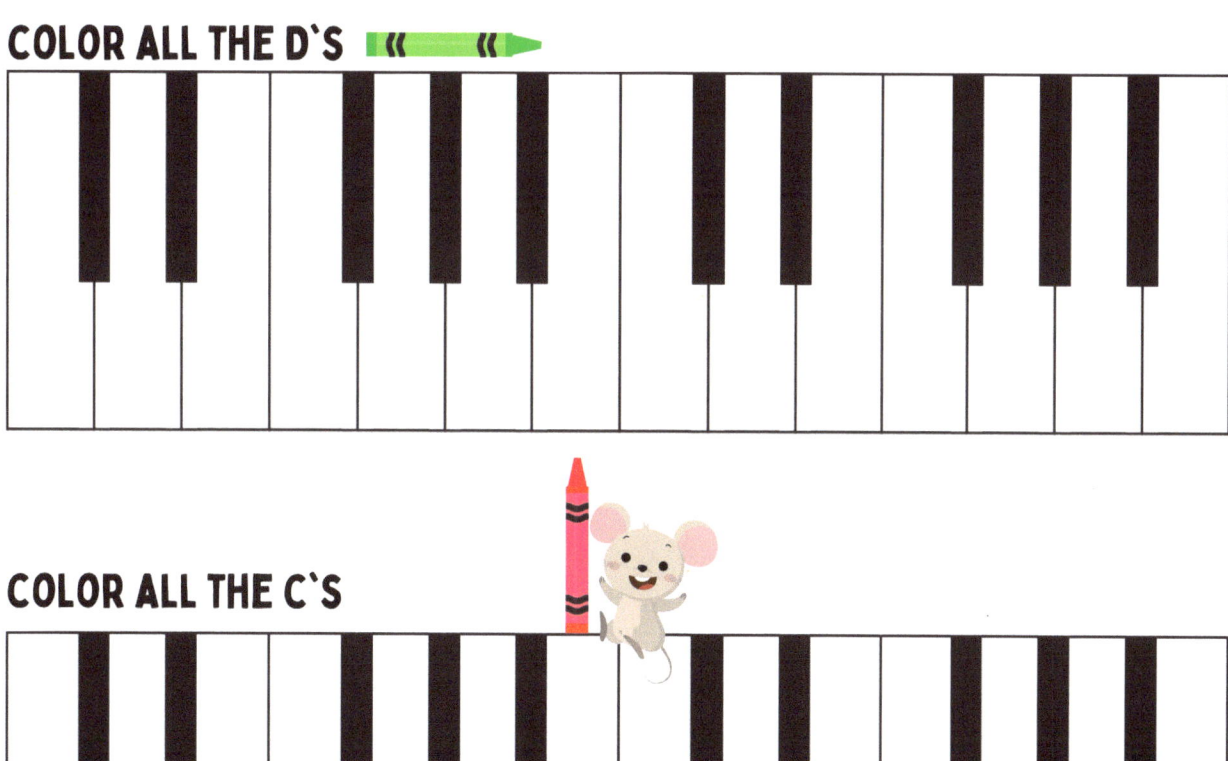

COLOR ALL THE C`S

Learn the music alphabet keyboard location in this video:

COLOR ALL THE F`S

SCHOOL DAYS, SCHOOL DAYS, GOOD OLD GOLDEN RULE DAYS,

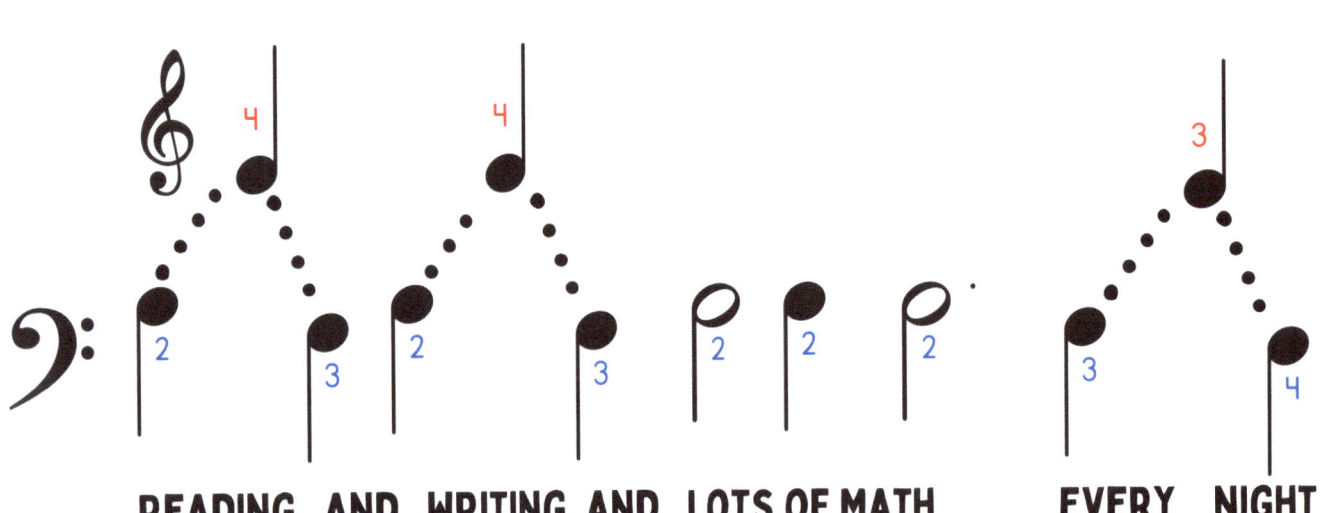

READING AND WRITING AND LOTS OF MATH, EVERY NIGHT

Need a practice reminder?

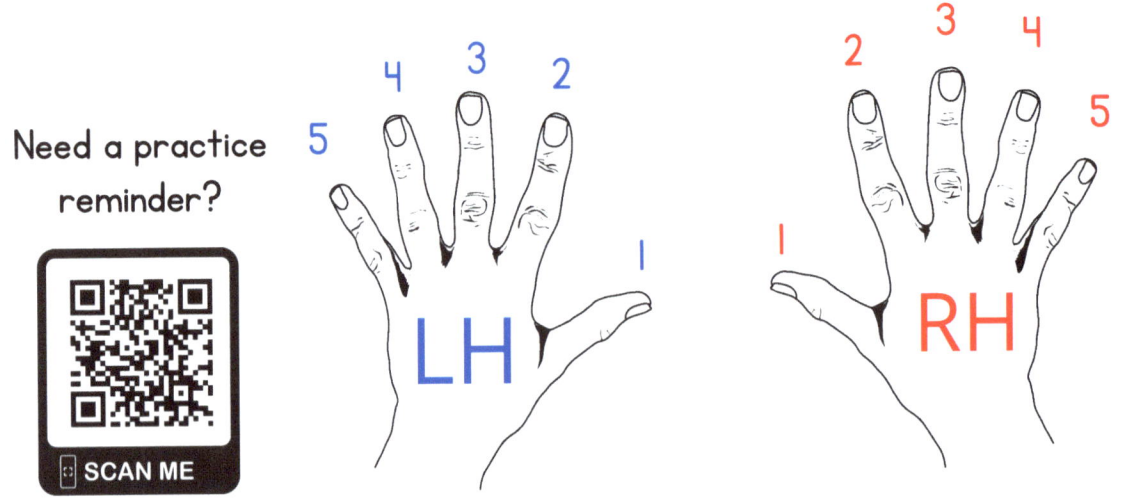

I HAVE TO TAKE A BATH! I LOVE TO PLAY AND
LEARN WITH MY FRIENDS, I LOVE SCHOOL DAYS!

C D E F G A B C D E F G A B

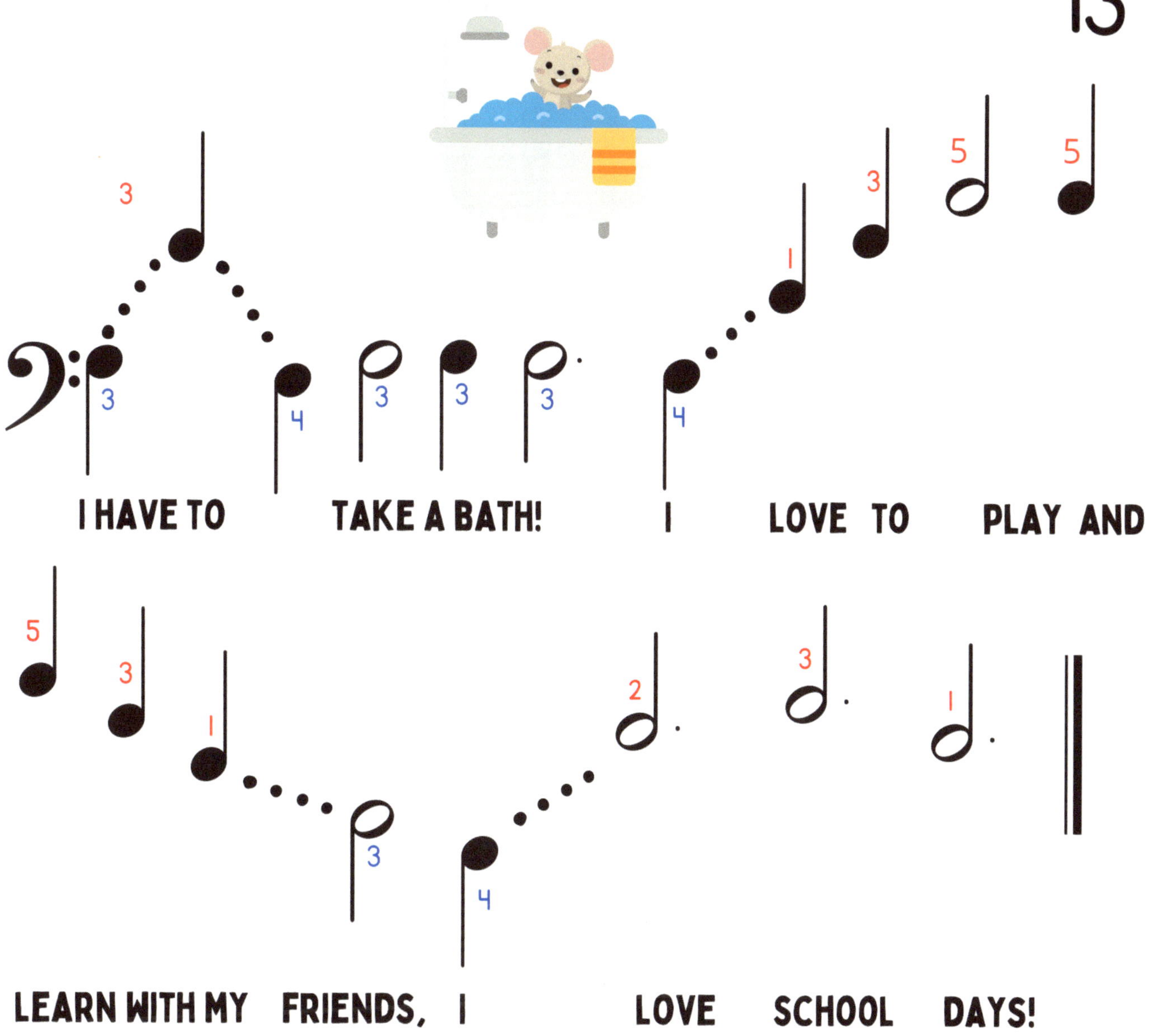

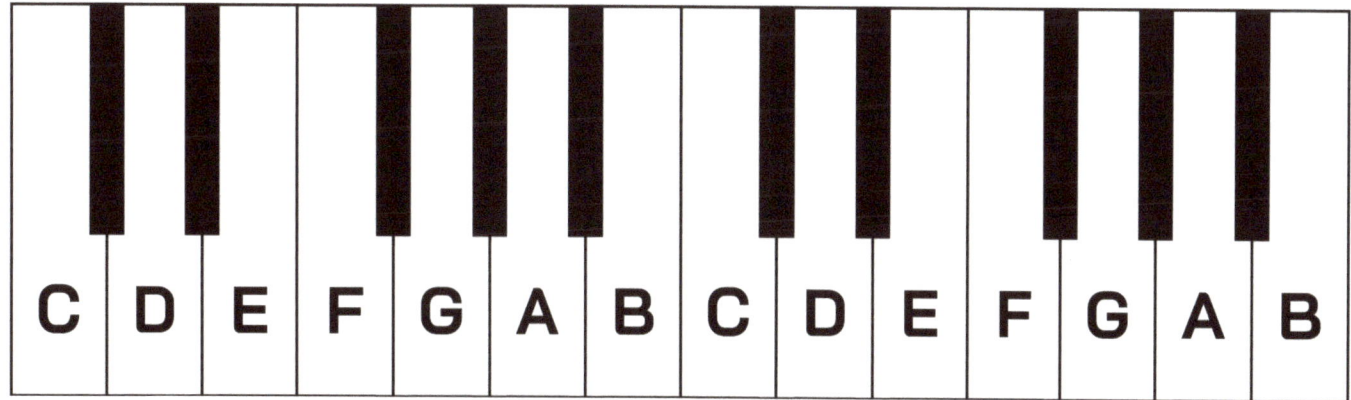

COLOR ALL THE E'S

COLOR ALL THE B'S

COLOR ALL THE C'S

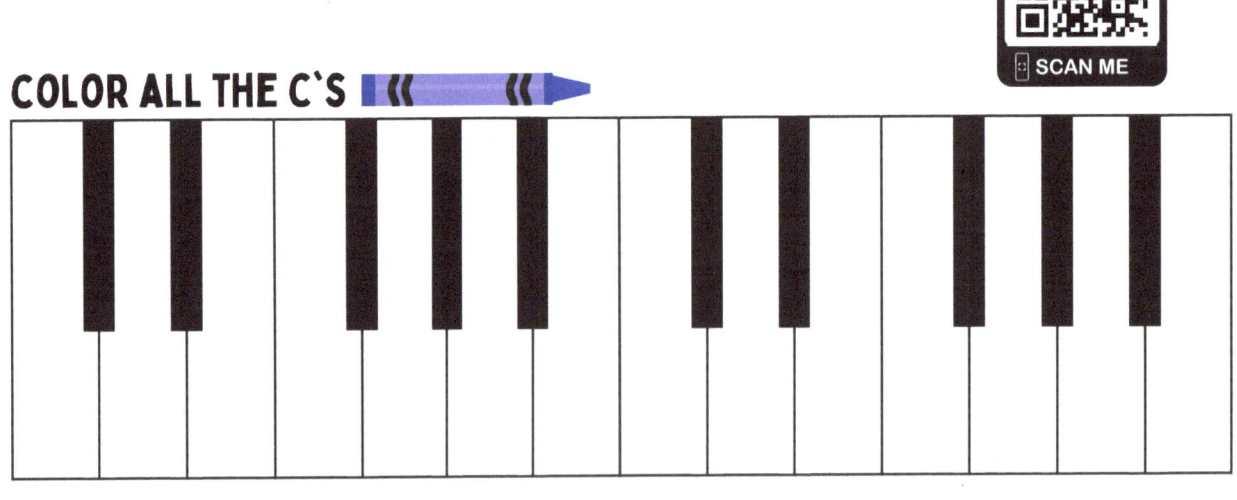

THE WHEELS ON THE BUS

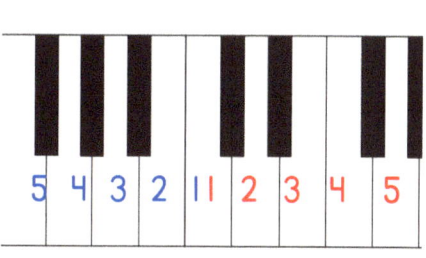
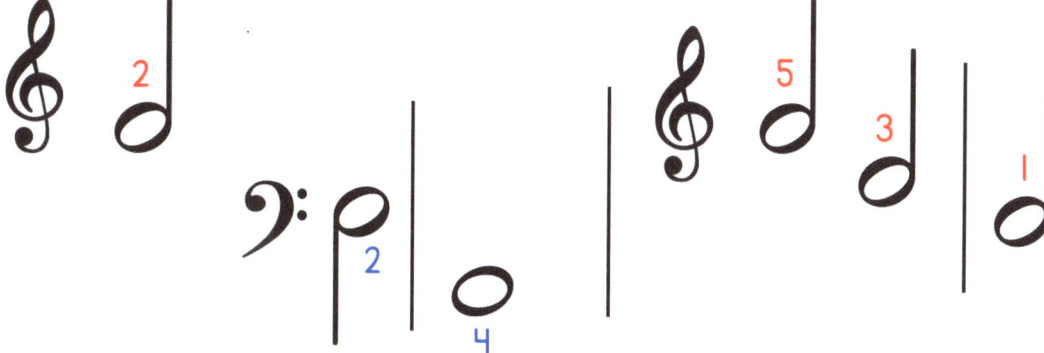
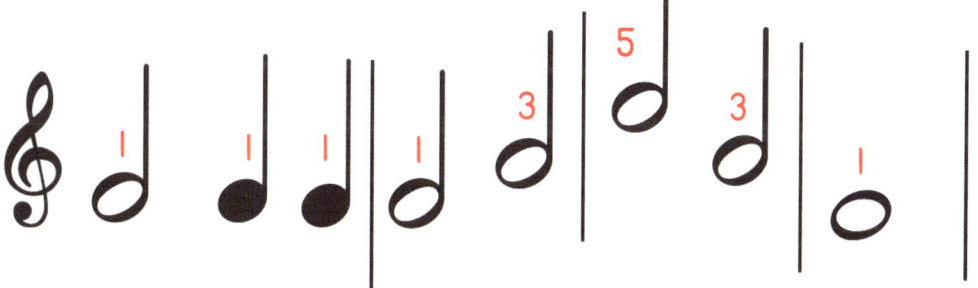

COLOR ALL THE D`S

COLOR ALL THE G`S

COLOR ALL THE A`S

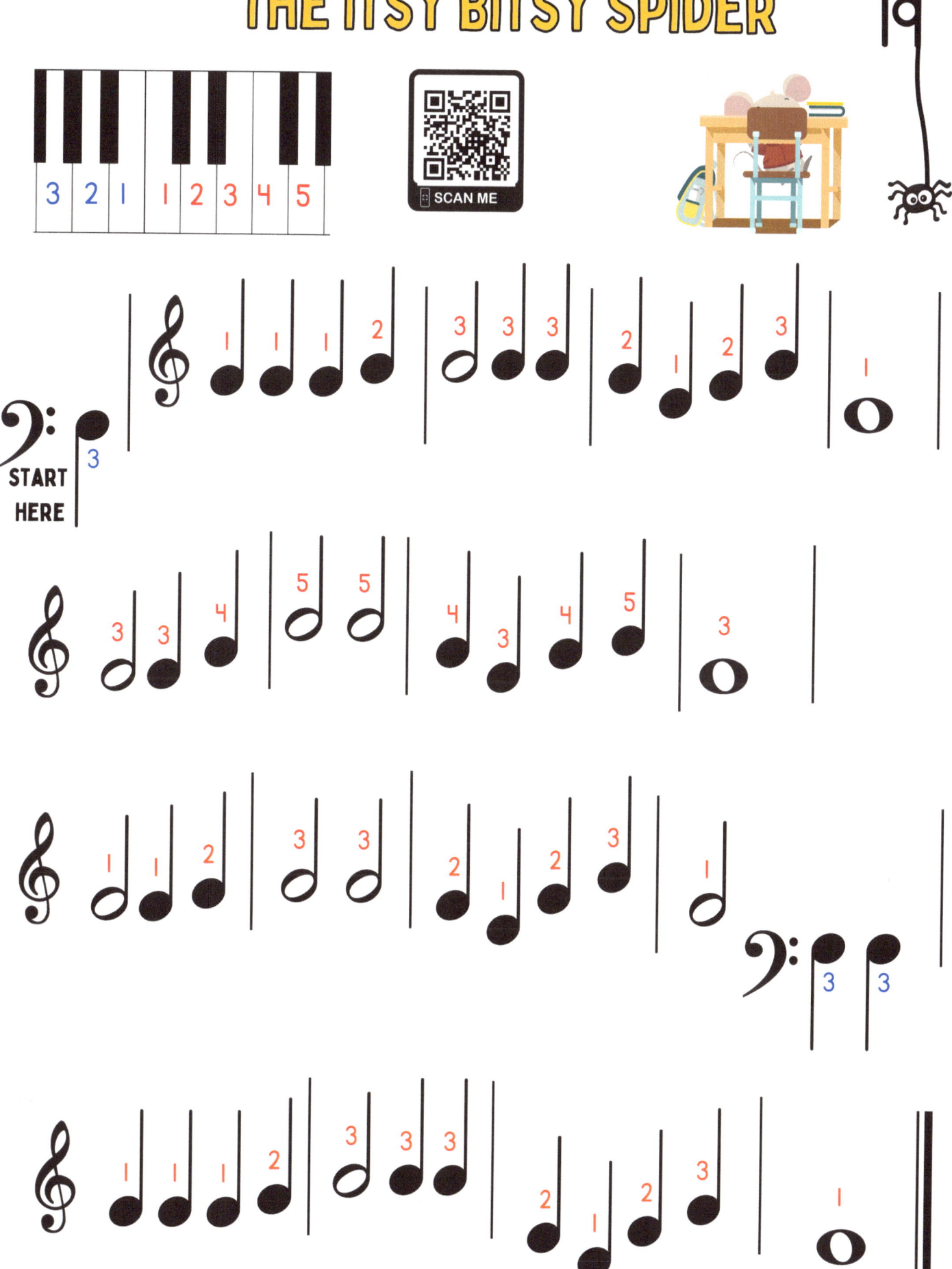

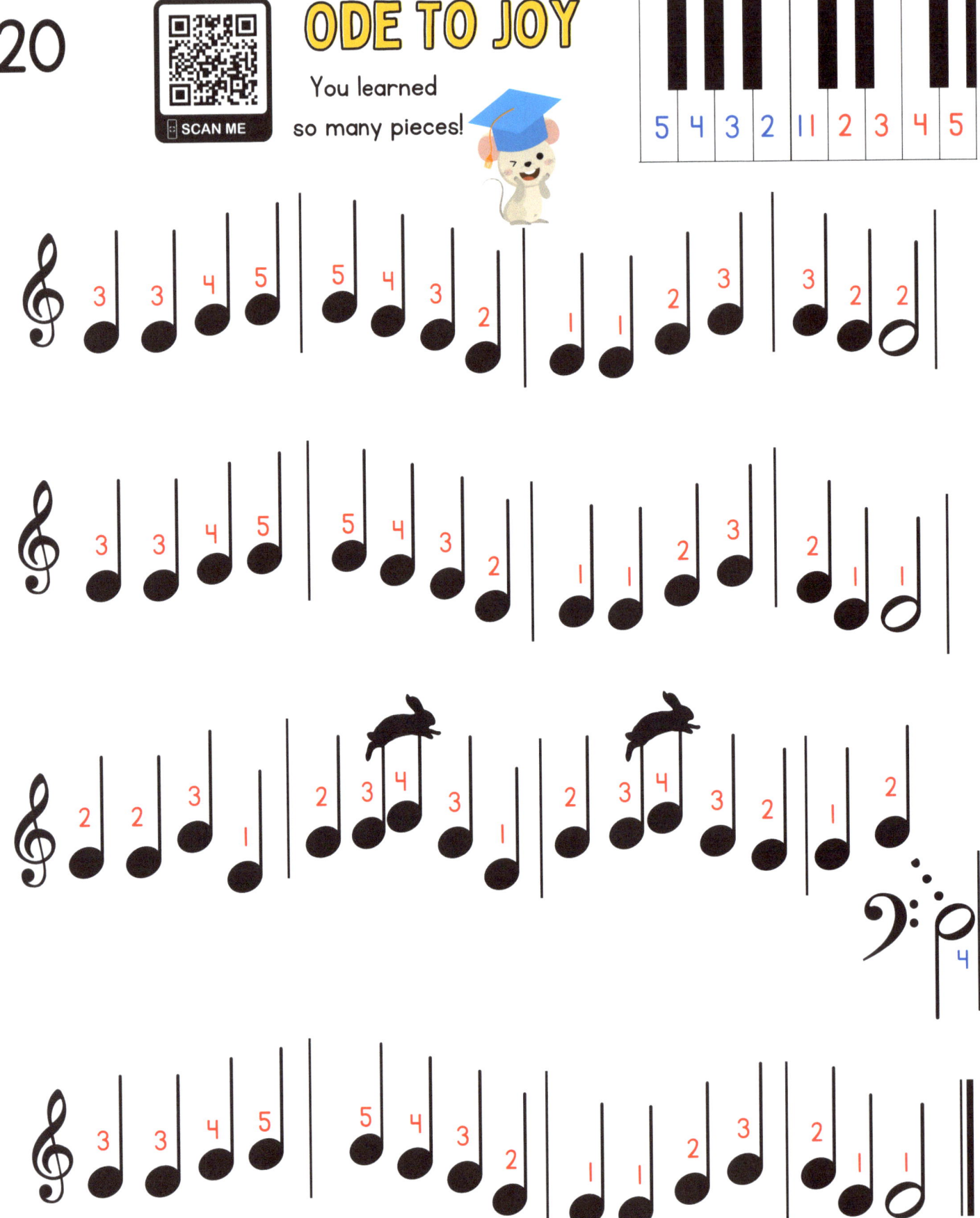

ALPHABET MAZE

Help Lucas the mouse find his way to the cheese through the music alphabet maze by connecting the notes in order:

C. JUDY NAILLON 2020 WWW.VIOLINJUDY.COM

BOOK LEVEL CHART FOR THE VERY FUN PIANO LIBRARY

PIANO GRADE	FUN PIANO LEVEL	MAIN CONCEPTS
PRE-READING FINGER LEARNING-EVERY FINGER LABELLED	A	USE FINGERS 1-5, BLACK KEY PIECES LEARN PIANO KEYS 4 BASIC RHYTHMS
PRE-READING DIRECTIONAL READING (LESS FINGER NUMBERS)	B	RUNNING BUNNY EIGHTH NOTES REINFORCE KEY NAMES
PRE-READING NOTE LETTERS IN NOTE HEADS	C	BEGIN TO LEARN NOTE NAMES AND KEYBOARD LOCATION
NOTE READING	D	ONLY LANDMARK NOTES WITH LETTERS AND FINGERS LABELLED
NOTE READING	E	DECODE WHERE HANDS GO ON THE PIANO KEYBOARD

C. JUDY NAILLON 2020 WWW.VIOLINJUDY.COM

Mrs. Judy Naillon, or "ViolinJudy" is a dedicated and enthusiastic independent piano and violin teacher, composer, and professional violinist. Her work consists of her large private music studio, as well as playing with her string quartet and Wichita Symphony Orchestra. She served as a church musician for over 20 years and is active in leadership in the musicians' union. She loves coming up with creative ideas to help both students and teachers be successful and blogs about it all at www.ViolinJudy.com and for Alfred's Music Publishers. When she is not writing new Violin books she loves spending time with her family and little dog Pom.

CERTIFICATE
OF ACHIEVEMENT

This awarded to :

----

for the achievement of the completion of:

Teacher   Date

www.ingramcontent.com/pod-product-compliance
Lightning Source LLC
Chambersburg PA
CBHW042126040426
42450CB00002B/91